Becoming a Christian

John Twisleton

Unless otherwise stated, scripture
quotations are taken from the New Revised
Standard Version of the Bible, Anglicised
edition, copyright © 1989, 1995 by the
Division of Christian Education of the
National Council of the Churches of Christ
in the United States of America.

ISBN: 9798352007860

Contents

Becoming a Christian

Thinking about becoming a Christian?

It's a great adventure and it can start today if you read through this booklet and make the decision. I've been one for years and find it draws me out of myself into a bigger scene rather like my picture under the viaduct draws your eye beyond me.

In becoming a Christian you will put faith in the immensity of God's love, recognise it's for you as well as for all people and things, turn from wrong, ask God into your life and get baptised into God's never-ending family.

The Bible is a guide to our reasoning. We need that guide because though we can think of God, God is, by definition, beyond us. Christianity is a revealed religion. It worships a God who's revealed in Jesus Christ. In the Bible we have a record of Christ's life, teaching, death and resurrection and the gift of the Holy Spirit. We also have this invitation which is to you and to all: 'Repent, and be baptized every one of you in the name of Jesus Christ so that your sins may be forgiven; and you will receive the gift of the Holy Spirit' (Acts 2:38)

Prayer, reaching out in heart and mind to God, is a second guide to becoming a Christian. Just as you can gaze beyond me in the picture into the extraordinary construction behind, I invite you to look beyond these pages and pray to God for help as you continue through this booklet. Though there are elaborate set prayers God can be accessed immediately one to one by anyone in their own words. I suggest you start by praying something like this prayer:

God give me a vision of you more to your dimensions and less to mine.
I can't see you but I sense you're alongside me as the ground of my being.

Please help me have more of you in my life as a Christian. Amen.

Clearing the path

Does God exist? The question may be an obstacle to your quest to become a Christian. My scientific career was one that engaged with what connects polymer molecules giving them their cohesion and non-stick properties. I saw the rationality of the material world and the connections I explored as evidence for a Creator who organised beforehand the connections I discovered in my research. God by definition is not a hypothesis that you can prove or disprove by knock down argument. How can we ever prove or disprove someone outside the observable? If you could observe God you would be above God and he would no longer be God! Blaming God, for example, for the existence of evil is trying to have it both ways. Believing in God who is greater than us can't exclude allowing him to have reasons for allowing suffering beyond our understanding.

Did Jesus exist? There are hundreds of references to Jesus in the New Testament which is the key source for his existence. In comparison with other documentation in ancient history, such copious records, written just decades after the alleged death of the personage, present very strong proof of his existence. Alexander the Great lived three centuries or so before Jesus and there is much less historical evidence for him dating close to his lifetime. Outside the Bible the Annals of Tacitus from the turn of the first century provide an unfavourable report of 'superstitious Christians' from the hand of one of the ancient world's most famous historians. A little later another historian, Suetonius, mentions the impact of Christ writing 'since the Jews were making disturbances at the instigation of [the so-called] Chrestus' the emperor expelled them from Rome. If Jesus did not exist, it makes Christianity more incredible than if he did. The story of Jesus has an extraordinary and consistent force about it that is hard to consign to mere invention.

Did Jesus rise from the dead? His teachings brought him rejection and crucifixion yet Jesus Christ is the only founder of a world religion without a grave. His resurrection is as well attested as many an event in history. The enigmatic tone of the accounts of Easter in the four gospels would be absent in any made-up tale. The role of women as witnesses - controversial at the time - would not have been included in any fabricated story. The new confidence found among frightened disciples confirms the resurrection as the founding truth of Christianity, because the transformation of a dejected, defeated group to a band of powerful witnesses to the resurrection would be inexplicable in human terms. It requires what they proclaimed (namely that Jesus had risen from the dead) to be true. Christ's resurrection is further evidenced in history by the newly formed Christian Church changing its weekly holy day from the Jewish Sabbath to Sunday, the day of Christ's rising. What a change that would have been for devout Jewish believers! The experience of meeting with Jesus as risen Lord is at the heart of Christianity's survival over 2000 years.

What about other faiths? Right from the beginning, holding loyalty to Jesus as the truth has not prevented Christians recognising what is true in other creeds as being also of him, since truth ultimately comes from the same divine source. Saying 'yes' to Jesus in becoming a Christian does not mean saying 'no' to everything about other faiths. Quite the opposite – it can mean saying 'yes, and...' to other faiths, which is a far more engaging and reasonable attitude. I say 'yes' to what Buddhists teach about detachment because Jesus teaches it and Christians often forget it. At the same time I must respectfully question Buddhists about the lack of a personal vision of God since I believe that Jesus is God's Son. I say 'yes' to what Muslims say about God's majesty, because sometimes Christians seem to domesticate God and forget his awesome nature. At the same time I differ with Muslims about how you gain salvation because I believe that Jesus is God's salvation gift and more than a prophet. The Christian faith points not to its own truth so much as to Jesus - whose truth is bigger than any religion. Being a

Christian is about being in a relationship with Jesus more than about holding to a set of beliefs.

Lord, thank you for the gift of reason by which I have examined objections to Christianity. See me through these, clear the pathway to you, as I prepare to welcome your search for me which balances mine for you. Amen.

God loves you

You are considering becoming a Christian. In doing so you will grasp a bigger scene than your life lived up to now has seen. You will grasp and be grasped by Love that brought being out of nothing, Jesus from a Virgin's womb and life out of death. The Maker anticipated the wrong use of free will by human beings - sin - and its destructive effect upon the world by a plan for its remaking executed 2000 years ago which you can be made part of. 'God, who is rich in mercy, out of the great love with which he loved us even when we were dead through our trespasses, made us alive together with Christ - by grace you have been saved - and raised us up with him' (Ephesians 2:4-6).

God made humans for friendship. Sin came in as a barrier to such friendship. By dying and rising for us Christ destroyed that barrier. Those who accept the risen Lord Jesus Christ - who become Christians - are raised by grace from their sins into friendship with God. In immense love God gave us life so every human being might receive the grace of the Holy Spirit if they so wish. To be a Christian is to have welcomed 'God's love ... poured into our hearts through the Holy Spirit that has been given to us' (Romans 5:5).

How do you welcome God's love? Go in your heart and mind to places where it is claimed eternity intersects time in Jesus Christ, such as the crib of Bethlehem, the cross of Calvary, the words of scripture, the font of baptism and the bread and wine of the eucharist. All these places are transparent to the immense love reaching down to us in Jesus Christ. A magnifying glass concentrates the rays of the sun into a burning knot of heat that can ignite things. If you look at the cross with faith in Christ as God's Son your heart will be set on fire by the ray of immense love that is concentrated there. 'The Son of God loved you and gave himself for you' (cf Galatians 2:20)

'For God so loved the world that he gave his only Son, so that everyone who believes in him may not perish but may have eternal life' (John 3:16).

Approach Jesus with faith in his divinity and you have to place his crucifixion at the climax of human history. It is an act of substitution: Jesus dies in our place so as to live in our place. The holiness of God, affronted by sin, demands a penalty which he himself provides. The shedding of the blood of God's Son Jesus Christ fulfils ancient sacrificial rites by providing the sinless victim who alone can expiate sin. As we read in Ephesians 'Christ loved us, giving himself up for us as an offering and a sweet smelling sacrifice to God' (Ephesians 5:2).

To put faith in the crucifixion of Jesus is to recognise a holy God who reaches out to us in love though we are sinners. In his holiness he cannot be reconciled to sin (Habakkuk 1:13a), but through the sacrifice of Jesus upon the Cross the horror and power of sin is potentially overcome and we are credited with God's holiness. The power of evil over humankind is overcome by the Cross, so Christ has been likened to a triumphant general who leads believers in his victory procession (2 Corinthians 2:14).

We come from God. We belong to God. We go to God. This is the Christian revelation, nothing man made but something revealed to us by God 'out of the great love with which he loved us' shown in historical events. These events invite the consideration of every human being. The rational mind can take us to Jesus, like a horse to water, but it cannot make us drink of him without faith.

Faith and reason are two wings on which the human spirit rises to God. Without the gift of faith we reason Jesus down to a level we can tolerate.

We conform Jesus to ourselves when the real business should be to conform ourselves to him. By the gift of faith Jesus complements our rational understanding so we can rise heavenwards and live lives open to the possibilities of God which go beyond our imagining.

God you sent Jesus your Son to die in my place, bearing my sins, so as to live in my place by the indwelling of your Spirit. Though such love is beyond my understanding, help me to put full trust in it so I can be a Christian. Amen.

Repent

I'm never happier than when helping people do business with God as here, seated in a mud confessional in the interior of Guyana, South America.

You have read up to this point how becoming a Christian means putting faith in God's love, recognising it's for you and turning from wrong before asking God into your life. You can't do this without repentance which is reaching up to God away from what's wrong in your life and makes your heart inhospitable to Christ.

The gravitational pull of God's love draws us up in competition with the gravitational field of evil in our souls, we call sin, which drags us down. Human beings are pulled down in the gravitational field of seven deadly sins: pride, anger, lust, envy, gluttony, avarice and sloth. Someone made up a mnemonic for these sins—'pale gas', indicating their deadly impact through a comparison to chlorine. The deadly sins weigh us down in different ways. For some of us, the heaviness is sloth, or laziness, especially as we get older. For others it's the weight of indulgence through gluttony, or the dead weight of pride that sinks so many of our relationships. Then we have avarice - greed, which can literally weigh us down! The downward gravity of sin affects us all. When we try to rise above it by our own efforts, we feel as if we are in the gym, trying to lift weights beyond our capacity. The more we try to lift ourselves, the heavier life feels. The gravitational field of God's love that lifts our lives can't be felt through our own efforts. It reaches down to offer us a hand up in Jesus and all he has done for us by his life, death and resurrection and the gift of the Holy Spirit. As we struggle with our relationships, insecurities and spiritual emptiness, we find ourselves caught by the gravitational lure of sin as if in quicksand. The more we struggle in our own strength to release ourselves, the deeper we go down. People caught in quicksand sink faster through gravity, the more they struggle to get out of it. They need an upward pull from outside themselves. Jesus does that for us when we repent and reach out to him.

How do you repent? You find your sins and bring them to God on your own or with the help of a trusted companion. This means examining your conscience in the light of God's Spirit starting with a prayer like this:

Come, Holy Spirit, and show me my sins so I can bring them to God to receive forgiveness and a new start as a Christian.

To identify your sins - some will cry out to you - think through this conscience examination of your failure to love God, neighbour and self:

Sins against God - distrust, ingratitude, blasphemy, disobedience...
Sins against neighbour - envy, gossip, hurtful acts, lack of consideration...
Sins against self - wrong pride, vanity, harbouring lust, gluttony, laziness...

Write the sins you identify on a piece of paper ready to take to God.

You can do this on your own, kneeling before a Cross or in church. Alternatively you could take the paper with your sins written on it to a Christian priest or lay leader who will pray with you and represent to you the welcoming love of God for sinners described by Jesus in the Bible:

'I will get up and go to my father, and I will say to him, "Father, I have sinned against heaven and before you... So he set off and went to his father. But while he was still far off, his father saw him and was filled with compassion; he ran and put his arms around him and kissed him... the father said... "Quickly, bring out a robe - the best one - and put it on him; put a ring on his finger and sandals on his feet. And get the fatted calf and kill it, and let us eat and celebrate; for this son of mine was dead and is alive again; he was lost and is found!' (Luke 15:18, 20, 22-24)

You could make an act of repentance by praying something like this prayer:

O God I recognise the immense love that brought your Son to die upon the Cross for me. I turn to you, Lord Jesus, and repent of my sins, especially.....
Please forgive my sins. Take my life and fill it with your love.
I make this prayer with confidence in the name of Jesus my Saviour. Amen.

Believe

It was here I stood as a teenager, under the Dome of Giggleswick School Chapel, to first declare my belief in Christ.

Paul and Silas in Acts 16:31 state that necessity for becoming a Christian: 'Believe on the Lord Jesus, and you will be saved'. This invitation focuses that of Peter in Acts 2:38 'Repent, and be baptized every one of you in the name of Jesus Christ so that your sins may be forgiven; and you will receive the gift of the Holy Spirit.'

Repent, believe, ask, receive – this is how we dispose ourselves to meet the Lord. That started for me at my confirmation, when I stood before the Bishop, in Giggleswick Chapel. It's also an ongoing process. I turn to Jesus, put faith in him, ask for and receive the Spirit. Then the Spirit shows me my need once again to turn to Jesus, believe in him, ask and receive from him – this is the day by day reality of my life!

You become a Christian when you put faith in God's love, having recognising it's for you, turn from wrong, ask for and receive God into your life and join God's family. The lost son in Jesus' parable prepared his confession of sin and returned to his father who 'ran and put his arms around him and kissed him' (Luke 15:20). Christianity, living as a Christian, is an accompanied journey so the context of your reading this booklet now becomes vital. The lost son repented and found forgiveness through the embrace of his father and joined a celebration meal. In the same way Christian enquirers come into Christian fellowship in the holy meal of bread and wine we call the Eucharist, Mass or Holy Communion. You are never alone as a believer. You may start your journey towards becoming a Christian through reading about it but to go further you need to get into conversation with practising Christians to be prepared for church membership through baptism, confirmation (in some traditions) and first Communion.

How do you believe? If your heart has been ignited to see Jesus as divine Saviour you already believe. If not, pray for a personal revelation to come through the Holy Spirit, like that which came to Peter when he said to Christ "You are the Messiah, the Son of the living God." And Jesus answered him, "Blessed are you... for flesh and blood has not revealed this to you, but my Father in heaven' (Matthew 16:16-17). It will help if, after research, you accept the existence and resurrection of Jesus as reasonable truths. You go on to make an act of faith like those of one who engaged with Jesus in Mark's Gospel: 'Jesus said to him... All things can be done for the one who believes... Immediately [he] cried out, "I believe; help my unbelief!"' (Mark 9:23-24)

To believe as a Christian is to acknowledge Christ as Son of God and Saviour who sends the Holy Spirit to dwell within us in the fellowship of the Church. Since the earliest days of Christianity the Apostles' Creed used at baptism has expressed fuller implications of acknowledging Christ's divinity in three paragraphs linked to belief in God as Father, Son and Holy Spirit:

I believe in God, the Father almighty, creator of heaven and earth.
I believe in Jesus Christ, his only Son, our Lord, who was conceived by the Holy Spirit, born of the Virgin Mary, suffered

under Pontius Pilate, was crucified, died, and was buried; he descended to the dead. On the third day he rose again; he ascended into heaven, he is seated at the right hand of the Father, and he will come to judge the living and the dead.

I believe in the Holy Spirit, the holy *catholic Church, the communion of saints, the forgiveness of sins, the resurrection of the body, and the life everlasting. Amen. (Church of England Common Worship text)

*Catholic here is not 'Roman Catholic' but 'universal' meaning the whole Church to which Anglicans, Orthodox and Protestants also have allegiance.

Here is a short act of faith built from joining Mark 9:24 and 2 Corinthians 4:6 into a simple prayer:

Lord, I believe; help my unbelief. Shine in my heart to give me the light of the knowledge of your glory in the face of Jesus Christ. Amen

Ask

This crucifix is one of the sights of Brighton in St Bartholomew's Church which has a stream of visitors calling in to pray. Becoming a Christian is about asking God for the Holy Spirit to be made a prayerful person. Once you repent of your sins and believe in Christ you are invited to ask God to supply your needs, especially for the Holy Spirit. Jesus taught us to pray for our needs 'for today' and made this graphic promise: 'Is there anyone among you who, if your child asks for a fish, will give a snake instead of a fish? Or if the child asks for an egg, will give a scorpion? If you then, who are evil, know how to give good gifts to your children, how much more will the heavenly Father give the Holy Spirit to those who ask him!' (Luke 11:11-13)

How do you ask God? You need to start voicing your needs to him which may seem strange at first. There are many unseen things in life that are really important. People who complain at God's invisibility don't complain they can't see electricity or the air around them. We see the *effect* of the wind even if we can't see it directly. Similarly though God is unseen he can be experienced by faith. Ask a married blind person if they believe in the love their spouse has for them. Not only can they not see their partner but they doubly can't see intangible love. They *know* the love their spouse has for them though. Similarly it is possible to experience God's presence and love without seeing him with our eyes. 'Blessed are those who have not seen and yet have come to believe' Jesus said (John 20:29). Faith, the letter to the Hebrews writes, is 'conviction of things unseen' (11:1).

Sitting, kneeling or standing, voice aloud your recognition of the unseen God and Father of Jesus, your sins, your belief and your desire for the love which is the Holy Spirit to flow through you - repent, believe, ask, receive!

What do you ask God for?

- To become a Christian, someone who knows God
- Forgiveness for your sins
- The Holy Spirit
- That your inner eyes open up to God's powerful yet invisible presence
- For a vision of God more to God's dimensions and less to your own
- Your needs to be sifted from your wants
- The joy of the Lord to be your strength (Nehemiah 8:10)
- A deeper sense of your need for God (Matthew 5:3)
- For the Bible to speak to you personally

- Spiritual companions to be sent your way
- To be led to the best Church for you in your locality
- To satisfy your thirst for God through baptism and Holy Communion
- That God will make you a better instrument of love, joy and peace
- 'The kingdom of this world to become the kingdom of our God and of his Christ' (Revelation 11:15)

Use the prayer Jesus taught us:

Our Father in heaven, hallowed be your name, your kingdom come, your will be done, on earth as in heaven.
Give us today our daily bread.

Forgive us our sins as we forgive those who sin against us. Lead us not into temptation but deliver us from evil.
For the kingdom, the power, and the glory are yours now and for ever. Amen.
(Church of England Common Worship text based on Matthew 6:9-15)

Faith is not a feeling. It's an ongoing decision to reach prayerfully towards God and be energised by him. By what the mystics call the 'eager dart of longing love' faith touches God and asks for the release of his possibilities into our situation. It is implied in the Bible that God is invisible to protect us from his glory. This invisibility serves our freedom to love without being manipulated. If God were visible that would dramatically affect our freedom to grow in pure love. By being invisible God can be with us without overwhelming us. He can stand at a distance to grant us freedom to make our own decisions including the decision to love him and our neighbour and ourselves.

O God, repenting of my sins, I put my trust in you and ask you to make room in my heart for the Holy Spirit. Amen.

Receive

Becoming a Christian is about opening up to a new dimension which is 'the light of the knowledge of the glory of God in the face of Jesus Christ' (2 Corinthians 4:6). Receiving the Holy Spirit is recognising the light of God shining through the circumstances of your life. Jesus Christ rose from the dead, appeared to his first disciples and then the appearances ceased. Though his physical body was taken from sight a second extraordinary event occurred which has made Jesus present across the world down through the ages. On the Jewish Feast of Pentecost, fifty days after his resurrection, light and fire from above descended upon the disciples and 'all of them were filled with the Holy Spirit' (Acts 2:4). From that day to now people who repent of their sins and put faith in Jesus can ask for and receive God's Spirit which opens up the new dimension of life possessed by a Christian helping us see God in all things. In the account of his baptism we read an example of how that dimension opens up as the Holy Spirit descended upon Jesus making him the Christ, literally 'the Anointed One'.

What is baptism? Through his death and resurrection Jesus has been authorised to share God's Spirit with us so that a Christian is one who shares in the anointing of the Anointed One. At his baptism Jesus heard his Father say 'You are my beloved Son' (Luke 3:22). Through his dying and rising Jesus has opened up the same privilege to Christians: to become God's *adopted* sons and daughters. This privilege links to his command that believers get washed with water in baptism so as to receive the promised Holy Spirit. Baptism, by pouring or immersion, is a symbolic drowning of our sins and rising to new life in the Holy Spirit. It is also the means of entering God's never-ending family, the Church, where life in the Holy Spirit is maintained by a second action commanded for the baptised by Jesus: sharing bread and wine as his body and blood to recall his sacrifice. Speaking of this means of receiving the Holy Spirit Jesus made strong emphasis: 'I tell you, unless you eat the flesh of the Son of Man and drink his blood, you have no life in you' (John 6:53)

How to receive the Holy Spirit

- 'Repent, and be baptized every one of you in the name of Jesus Christ so that your sins may be forgiven; and you will receive the gift of the Holy Spirit.' (Acts 2:38)
- Look back through this booklet reflecting upon God's love for you and his call to repent and believe, ask for and receive that love

- Identify your sins by thinking through your failure to love God, neighbour and self
- Confess your sins to God on your own or with a helper
- Take opportunity to read through the Apostles' Creed and sort any difficulties you have about it with a trusted helper
- Ask God for the Holy Spirit
- Ask God to guide you, maybe through a trusted helper, to the best Church for you in your locality
- Sign up for Christian Initiation

What is Christian Initiation? It is becoming a Christian, the subject of this booklet, and can be achieved in three minutes on the next page. As the prayer there indicates Christian initiation is inseparable from church membership or desire for it. Once you welcome God's love in prayer you are a Christian even if you remain unbaptised. Early Christian martyrs are honoured though they died whilst still preparing for baptism. Such preparation is 'Christian Initiation' in the plain sense, a season of prayer with the opportunity to receive teaching about the creed, sacraments, commandments and prayer before baptism, confirmation and admission to share the bread and wine at the eucharist. The seven weeks before Easter we call Lent originate from a common practice of baptising at Easter after those weeks of prayer and instruction (catechising) accompanied by church members. Those of us who are baptised experience Christian initiation as an ongoing reality. Teachers train to become teachers by teaching. Christians are baptised to keep dying daily to sin and daily receiving the Holy Spirit. To fully receive the Holy Spirit and be formally initiated as a Christian you should enrol in a local church. If you were baptised as an infant this is the opportunity to make the most of this.

Lord Jesus, I welcome your invitation: Come to me, all you that are weary and are carrying heavy burdens, and you will find rest for your souls. Amen.

Prayer to become a Christian

God's love

Lord Jesus Christ,
truly God yet truly human,
you loved me and gave yourself for me.
I put my trust in your love.

Repent

I repent of my sins, especially...

Believe

I put my faith in you so that
your Father can be my Father.

Receive

I ask for the share in your anointing
as Christ by the Holy Spirit
that you promise in the Bible.

Church membership

In faith I receive from you
[in anticipation of my baptism].

I hunger for you,
my Lord and God,
my food and my drink,
at the *eucharist.

Self offering

I give myself to you.
Take me and use me,
as a Christian,
to live and work
to God's praise and service
in the fellowship of the Church,
which is your body,
the fullness of God
who fills all in all.

Hope of glory

God be praised,
God's kingdom come,
God's will be done,
in the company of saints
on earth
and in heaven
now and for ever.
Amen.

*Eucharist meaning 'thanksgiving' is the main act of Christian worship recalling Christ, also known as Mass, Liturgy, Communion or Breaking of Bread in which participants receive bread and wine as Christ's body and blood.

Following through

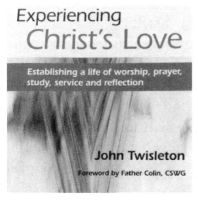

Experiencing Christ's Love

Establishing a life of worship, prayer, study, service and reflection

John Twisleton

Foreword by Father Colin, CSWG

As you prayed to become a Christian the hand of God reached down to you and now invites you to grasp it with your own hand, its five digits symbolising **five loves** commended in Christ's summary of the Old Testament Law: "You shall love the Lord your God with all your heart, and with all your soul, and with all your mind.' This is the greatest and first commandment. And a second is like it:

'You shall love your neighbour as yourself"
Matthew 22:37f.

In this summary teaching Jesus implies worship and prayer are to be seen as the heart and soul of our love for God. He implies, though, that without study engaging the mind with divine teaching that love will be ill formed, and without service, love of neighbour, and reflection, loving care of self, our loving God is a delusion.

Those five commitments - **worship, prayer, study, service, reflection** - can be seen as a hand that can grasp the hand of God reaching down to us in Jesus Christ to raise us into his praise and service with all the saints, an image of the grace (or favour) of God towards us. Following Jesus as Christians, our response to God's love finds expression in a rule of life in the power of the Holy Spirit so we worship on Sunday, pray every day, study the Bible, serve our neighbour and reflect upon our lives confessing our sins.

In worship the Lord's people gather on the Lord's Day around the Lord's table. The Sunday eucharist is 'the hour of Jesus' in which we soak in his presence in word and sacrament to be refreshed as his disciples. Meeting Jesus in the eucharist goes beyond spiritual refuelling though. 'Proclaiming the Lord's death until he comes' has global and cosmic impact. The memorial sacrifice that is the eucharist lifts participants into the worship that began with angels before ever the world was made and will continue with angels and 'just people made perfect' (Hebrews 12:22) into eternity.

In prayer we respond to the joyful, loving goodness of God as individuals. God loves us through and through and inspires in us the discipline of daily prayer which is loving God in heart and soul. Prayer is a lifting of the soul or inner being to God inspired by God, part of the love offering that responds to the extravagance of his love more fully with worship, study, service and reflection. Like God's presence, prayer is invisible, an activity of the soul, though as with God it can find a voice. Without that activity life turns soul-less in the sense it loses connection with God who is the ground of our being.

In study of the Bible and the Christian tradition we are empowered. Through it worship is offered with fuller understanding, prayer kindled as God's word comes alive, service inspired by the observation of need and self knowledge deepened through the study we call conscience examination. Study enlarges our horizon, raises our perspective and catalyses praise. There is no Word of God without power so the more we familiarise ourselves with what God speaks to us in the Bible the more our lives get empowered.

In service we commit to live, as God lives, in the present moment open to serve those in need which is both a surprising and self-forgetful business. Whereas rules of worship, prayer, study and reflection are relatively simply organised, a rule of service is more complicated. Christian service isn't something organised quantitatively since it's primarily qualitative. It's the work of the Lord inseparable from the Lord of the work, which means making sure our hearts are in it as best we can.

In reflection we are regular in self examination to keep ourselves on the right path and not miss out on God's invitations to us. Being a Christian is being open to the Holy Spirit's guidance and that of fellow Christians so as to find God's future for yourself and venture towards it. So much of life draws on our capacity to reflect, adjust and make sacrifice. In adjusting we find consolation in a God who has adjusted to humanity through the gift of Jesus, his suffering, resurrection and the gift of the Holy Spirit.

More in John Twisleton Experiencing Christ's Love (BRF, 2017)

May you know the love of Christ that surpasses knowledge, so that you may be filled with all the fullness of God. Ephesians 3:19

Books by the author

A History of St Giles Church, Horsted Keynes

Besides being the burial place of former UK Prime Minister Harold Macmillan (1894-1986) and mystic ecumenist Archbishop Robert Leighton (1611-1684) St Giles, Horsted Keynes has association with the history of Sussex back to the 8th century. As 53rd Rector (2009-2017) John Twisleton wrote this illustrated history with the assistance of church members.

Baptism - Some Questions Answered

Illustrated booklet on infant baptism used across the Anglican Communion. It explains the commitments involved in baptising a baby, challenges hypocrisy and attempts to clear up a number of misunderstandings in popular culture about what baptism is all about.

Christianity - Some Questions Answered

This booklet for Christian enquirers attempts dialogue between Christianity and its contemporary critics. A brief inspection of Christian faith clarifies both its unique claims and its universal wisdom so they can be seen and owned more fully.

Confession - Some Questions Answered

Illustrated booklet explaining the value of sacramental confession as an aid to spiritual growth. It commends confession as a helpful discipline serving people as they struggle against sin and guilt and seek to renew church membership.

Elucidations - Light on Christian controversies

As an Anglocatholic priest who experienced a faith crisis enlarging God for him, John Twisleton, former scientist, sheds light on thoughtful allegiance to Christianity in the 21st century condensing down thinking on controversial topics ranging from self-love to unanswered prayer, Mary to antisemitism, suffering to same sex unions, charismatic experience to the ordination of women, hell to ecology and trusting the Church, a total of twenty five essays.

Empowering Priesthood

This book is an enthusiastic presentation about the gift and calling of the ministerial priesthood. It argues that the choosing and sending of priests is vital to the momentum of mission and that their representation of Christ as priest, prophet and shepherd is given to help build love, consecrate in truth and bring empowerment to the whole priestly body of Christ.

Entering the Prayer of Jesus

Audio CD and booklet prepared by John Twisleton with the Diocese of Chichester and Premier Christian Radio providing spiritual wisdom from across the whole church. Contains audio contributions from Pete Greig (24-7 Prayer), Jane Holloway (Evangelical Alliance), Christopher Jamison (Worth Abbey), Molly Osborne (Lydia Fellowship) and Rowan Williams (Archbishop of Canterbury).

Experiencing Christ's Love

A wake up call to the basic disciplines of worship, prayer, study, service and reflection helpful to loving God, neighbour and self. Against the backdrop of the message of God's love John Twisleton presents a rule of life suited to enter more fully the possibilities of God.

Fifty Walks from Haywards Heath

Sub-titled 'A handbook for seeking space in Mid Sussex' this book celebrates the riches of a town at the heart of Sussex. Through detailed walk routes with schematic illustrations John Twisleton outlines routes from one to thirteen miles with an eye to local history and replenishment of the spirit.

Firmly I Believe

Forty talks suited to Christians or non-Christians explaining the creed, sacraments, commandment and prayer engaging with misunderstandings and objections to faith and its practical expression. Double CD containing 40 easily digested 3 minute talks accompanied by reflective music with full text in the accompanying booklet.

Forty Walks from Ally Pally

John Twisleton explores the byways of Barnet, Camden, Enfield and Haringey with an eye to green spaces, local history and a replenishment of the spirit. The routes, which vary in length between one mile and twenty miles, exploit the public transport network, and are well designed for family outings. The author provides here a practical handbook for seeking space in North London.

Guyana Venture

The beauty and challenge of Guyana, formerly British Guiana, has drawn a succession of missionaries from the Church of England to South America. 'Guyana Venture' is framed by John Twisleton's service there. Mindful of the ambiguities of the colonial past he writes proudly of the Church of England venture especially its helping raise up indigenous priests to serve Guyana's vast interior.

Healing - Some Questions Answered

An examination of the healing ministry with suggested ecumenical forms for healing services. The booklet addresses divine intervention, credulity, lay involvement, evil spirits and the healing significance of the e-7—7-ucharist.

Holbrooks History

Illustrated booklet compiled by John Twisleton with members of St Luke's Church, Holbrooks in Coventry about their parish and its church. It describes a multicultural community that has welcomed Irish, West Indian, Eastern European and Indian workers over the last century. The book includes dramatic pictures from the Second World War when the community and its church suffered bomb damage.

Meet Jesus

In a world of competing philosophies, where does Jesus fit in? How far can we trust the Bible and the Church? What difference does Jesus make to our lives and our communities? Is Jesus really the be all and end all? John Twisleton provides a lively and straightforward exploration of these and other questions pointing to how engaging with Jesus expands both mind and heart.

Moorends and its Church

Illustrated booklet telling the tale of the Doncaster suburb of Moorends from the sinking of the pit in 1904 to the 1984-5 mining dispute under the theme of death and resurrection. It includes a community survey of the needs of the elderly, young people and recreational and spiritual needs.

Pointers to Heaven

Completed at the height of COVID 19 this book condenses philosophical, theological and life insight into ten pointers to heaven troublesome to materialists: goodness, truth and beauty pointing to perfection alongside love, suffering, holy people and visions pointing beyond this world. If heaven makes sense of earth it is presented as doing so through such pointers, complemented by scripture, the resurrection and the eucharist, preview of the life to come.

Thirty walks from Brighton Station

A practical handbook for exploring the city and its surrounds reaching beyond the daytripper's duo of Pier and Pavilion to two hundred and sixty six sights with commentary on many of these. John Twisleton describes his motivation being linked, as a historian, to love for Brighton & Hove, as a walker, to the replenishment of body, mind and spirit attained in that pursuit and as an environmentalist to serving recreation with low carbon footprint.

Using the Jesus Prayer

The Jesus Prayer of Eastern Orthodoxy, 'Lord Jesus Christ, Son of God, have mercy on me a sinner' offers a simple yet profound way of deepening spiritual life. John Twisleton gives practical guidance on how to use it outlining the simplification of life it offers.

More at Twisleton.co.uk

Printed in Great Britain
by Amazon